Nebula

my guide to the solar system

CHERRY LAKE PRESS

Published in the United States of America by Cherry Lake Publishing
Ann Arbor, Michigan
www.cherrylakepublishing.com

Reading Adviser: Beth Walker Gambro, MS, Ed., Reading Consultant, Yorkville, IL
Book Design: Jennifer Wahi
Illustrator: Jeff Bane

Photo Credits: © NASA images/Shutterstock.com, 5, 17; © PIA14444/NASA, 7; © nienora/Shutterstock.com, 9; © PIA15415/NASA, 11; © PIA03606/NASA, 13; © PIA13028/NASA, 15; © Artsiom P/Shutterstock.com, 19; © AstroStar/Shutterstock.com, 21; © Outer Space/Shutterstock.com, 23; Cover, 2-3, 16, 18, 22, 24, Jeff Bane

Cherry Lake Press is an imprint of Cherry Lake Publishing Group.

Library of Congress Cataloging-in-Publication Data

Names: Devera, Czeena, author. | Bane, Jeff, 1957- illustrator.
Title: Nebula / by Czeena Devera ; illustrated by Jeff Bane.
Description: Ann Arbor, Michigan : Cherry Lake Publishing, [2022] | Series:
   My guide to the solar system | Audience: Grades K-1
Identifiers: LCCN 2021036741 (print) | LCCN 2021036742 (ebook) | ISBN
   9781534199064 (hardcover) | ISBN 9781668900208 (paperback) | ISBN
   9781668905968 (ebook) | ISBN 9781668901649 (pdf)
Subjects: LCSH: Nebulae--Juvenile literature.
Classification: LCC QB855.2 .D48 2023 (print) | LCC QB855.2 (ebook) | DDC
   523.1/135--dc23
LC record available at https://lccn.loc.gov/2021036741
LC ebook record available at https://lccn.loc.gov/2021036742

Printed in the United States of America
Corporate Graphics

table of contents

About the author: Czeena Devera grew up in the red-hot heat of Arizona surrounded by books. Her childhood bedroom had built-in bookshelves that were always full. She now lives in Michigan with an even bigger library of books.

About the illustrator: Jeff Bane and his two business partners own a studio along the American River in Folsom, California, home of the 1849 Gold Rush. When Jeff's not sketching or illustrating for clients, he's either swimming or kayaking in the river to relax.

I'm a nebula. I'm found in outer space.

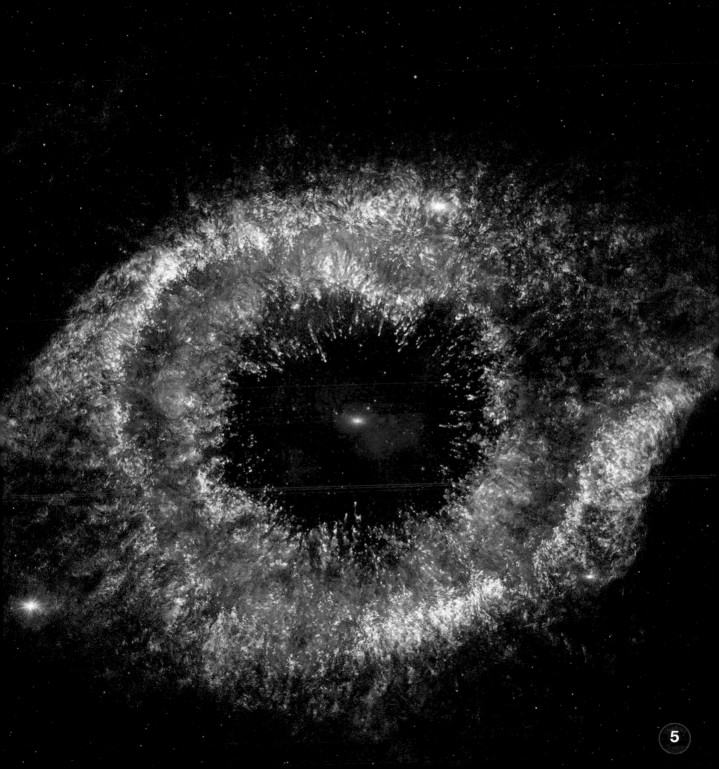

I'm a large collection of dust and gas.

I exist in an area called "**interstellar** space." This is the space between stars.

I **vary** in shape, size, and even color!

There are many of us in space. Most of us form from a star's explosion. This explosion is called a **supernova**.

There are others of us that are called "star **nurseries**." This is because we help new stars form.

The closest nebula is 700 **light-years** from Earth. That's really far!

Scientists love to photograph us. They use special cameras to take pictures.

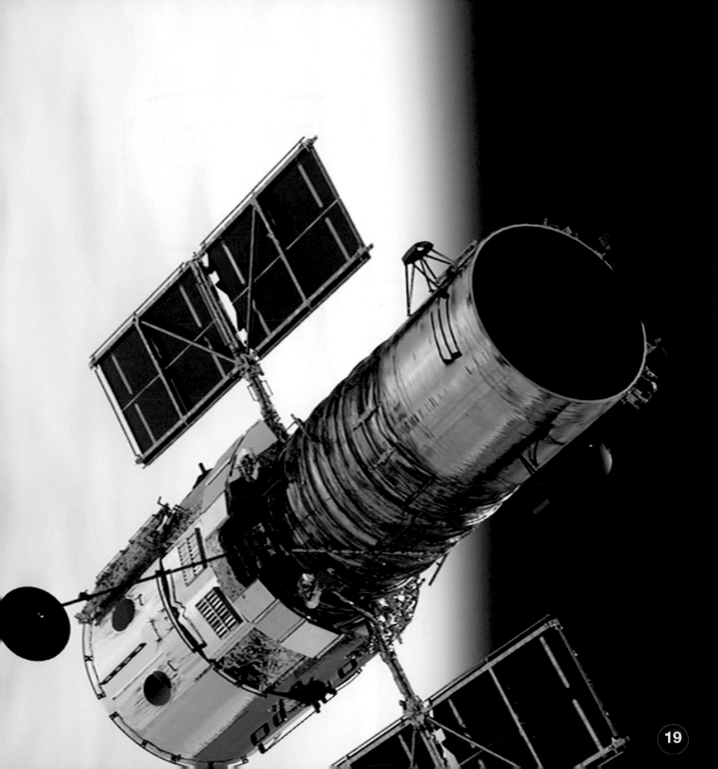

Most of us need special **telescopes** to be seen. But sometimes you can see us by looking up into the night sky.

Scientists are still studying me.
There's so much more to learn!

glossary

interstellar (in-tuhr-STEH-luhr) located or taking place among the stars

light-years (LITE-yeerz) distances traveled by light in a year

nurseries (NUHR-suh-reez) places where young things are grown or cared for

scientists (SYE-uhn-tists) people who study nature and the world we live in

supernova (soo-puhr-NOH-vuh) the explosion of a star

telescopes (TEH-luh-skohpz) instruments that make distant objects seem larger and closer

vary (VAIR-ee) to change or be different

index